Girl Shedding Glass Pieces

Devon Lopes

BookLeaf Publishing

India | USA | UK

Presentation by *BookLeaf Publishing*

Web: www.bookleafpub.com

E-mail: info@bookleafpub.com

ISBN: 9789363304376

First edition 2024

ACKNOWLEDGEMENT

I would not have found the courage to share my stories or known my power in telling them if it were not for the Goddesses of Sacramento. To my treasured community of Goddess Night Out: thank you.

PREFACE

I once read about accounts of a psychiatric disorder in Europe from the 15th to 17th centuries in which people feared they were made of glass and would shatter into pieces. The phenomenon was coined "the glass delusion".

A news article from 2007 told of a 12-year-old girl from Lebanon who cried glass tears. The girl said she woke up one morning feeling pain in her eye and felt something coming out. The girl would shed 7 to 8 pieces of glass from her eye daily. Her parents claimed it was a miracle from God. Doctors believed the girl's father broke a glass near his daughter's face a few months earlier.

In 2019, a 22-year-old Armenian woman was reportedly shedding glass from her eyes. She would "weep" up to 50 pieces a day. People in her village told investigative reporters that the glass pieces appeared shortly after the woman's son smashed a glass vase near her head. Doctors accused her of Munchausen syndrome.

A scientific journal reported a case of a 16-year-old girl shedding 10 to 15 glass pieces from her upper and lower limbs every day. The girl was a high school dropout from a small rural town with difficult family relationships. After extensive medical tests and therapy, doctors determined her diagnosis to be "Dermatitis artefacta". In other words, it was a non-malicious falsified condition caused by self-inflicted trauma.

Factitious dermatitis is more common in females than males with a peak age of representation during the second to third decade of life. Early life adversities including abuse and neglect during childhood increase the risk of these disorders. All of these accounts obsessed me; why glass...?

Glass can do many things: let light in, warp your view, shatter and injure you. It can be rigid, heavy, fragile, colored, molded, or smooth. It has value. It can be for luxury, art, decor, or function. It preserves and reflects. It withstands heat and time. It's a bitch to have embedded in your skin. It can sparkle and shine. One way or another, glass makes you feel something. Maybe that's all these girls were trying to do.

I am the girl.

These words are my glass pieces.

I hope they make you feel something too.

Give Me a Smiling Death*
(Life is Crushing Me)

Smile!
With your whole face
Don't be afraid of crow's feet
Any moment we'll be extricated
From this extended period of crush injury
Let's show blood through the gaps in our teeth
Instead of saying "sunny day" when we meet
Let's dance as we pass on the street
Fuck a chuckle
Let's chat heartache
Laugh at betrayal
Paint our faces in summer-freckles-of-grief
Comment on how well they're filling in
Smile so hard we see stars
Our cheeks burn
And we can't breathe
Let's see how far we can stretch this skin
Smile now
Big as you can
Before you rest
Pale in satin
And they request one painted in
[Smiling Death* is a prehospital phenomenon
caused by Crush Syndrome. It occurs when a

person experiences large areas of tissue damage from a compression injury. Upon removal of the crushing force high levels of potassium enter circulation and cause cardiac arrhythmias leading to sudden death. The person is happy to be rescued but dies so suddenly afterwards that they die smiling.]

For Beauty's Sake

How young were you when you started hating
your body?
I'll bet it was one of two times:
When your power began to show
As in body hair, blood, stretch marks, boobs
Or in your grandmother's womb

I was raised on Christian values
And one twisted fundamental truth:
For beauty's sake it's okay to lie

Not allowed to shame anyone else
But subtly encouraged to hate myself

The expectation set by women in my life
(save a few who were openly chastised)
Was to hide what set me apart from the
media-portrayed-mainstream

My hidden parts were not much different
From most other human beings
But I didn't know

Because everyone takes their chance to change
And we all walk around being fake
For beauty's sake

Of Beauty and Strangeness

We're not the same, you and me
I was made from a cloth cut deep
Printed from passion and tragedy
You sweetly sew someone else's dreams
Buttons neat as Q's and P's
But my design is splitting at the seams
I'm busy
Binding tattered pieces into mosaic motif
Finding crimson feathers for my funeral next
week
Yes, I'll die in this fashion again
Frothing fringe and anger
Frayed by the pain the world is in
Don't look confused when I rise making rags
look rich
Don't tell me fury is the new black
If you can only imagine it

Beauty without strangeness doesn't exist
Not
Everything
Fits

The whole purpose of this physical you is
expression

Babe, listen!
How many summers do you even have left?
Wear the outfit
Follow your bliss
Blow kisses to haters
Be the baddest bitch

If Only We Could Remember

Remember the names of flowers and trees
The number and shape of their leaves
Their scent — their true scent
Not something sprayed from a can

If only we knew where they grow and when
If we spoke to them
Heard them
Made friends

If we stopped reading captions to look at the
land
What's left of it
Stopped watching the frame in our hands
Paid attention instead to which petals feel like
velvet
Which stems make good thread

If we could remember how bees dance
Wait patiently to see a hummingbird land
We wouldn't need sources or likes for things to
make sense

She understands the world better without words
She's felt Yarrow fresh and full

Fallen into it face-first and brought it home in
her hair
Watered it
Watched it die — not in sadness
That's just life

Not even language lives forever
Something in her knows that words are not
enough
Where this world is headed
We won't need to talk
We'll need to feel
We'll need to love

You Say Spinster Like It's a Bad Thing

Webs in sunlight
Delicately spun in a corner
For function and strength
Like silver hairs of sage
Tucked behind an ear
Or lace sewn inside a pocket
Where you only catch a glimpse
In just the right light
Of the beauty hiding there
Of the precious value held
In its labile cradle
Like dewdrops
Or a wise woman
Waiting
Like life
Fading

I'm Just a Tulip

Bound to bloomed
Perked to drooped
Hot pink to faded fuchsia
Petals pleat then drop
Every stage more beautiful than the last

Like a sunset
Or wearing your grandmother's jewelry
Savoring a taste that lingers
As long as you possibly can

Sometimes a flower is just a flower
A moment beautiful just because
Tulips don't need reason to bloom
Only sunlight, water, and love
Me too

It's Dark Here Without You

I chase the light each day
Till I'm breathless and weak
To find what I'm not looking for
Fall in love accidentally
Spin off into timelines
That better suit me
You suit me
Let's get sewn up
Trés chic
Our fingers interlaced
Our necks pressed together
Our shadows
Eyes
And lips
All dancing
In the light I chase

Two Desert Hearts

Like ours, pressed together
Everywhere we went
Two shy desert blooms
Open for a short time
Two fragile Joshua Trees
You shouldn't touch

Did you notice them?
In the stars
In the clouds
In a pair of tiny paws
Memorialized in clay
In the silhouette of two ravens
Perched side by side
Like ours, still lonely in a way

Remember the two hearts
Made from four seeds
In the core of my apple
I showed you on the plane
But ate them
Instead of taking a photo

Remember the heart we made
Or tried to

With our shadows
Like the kids do
But my elbow wouldn't bend that way

Remember the paper glasses
That turned every point of light
Into rainbow hearts
Like ours, magic in the moment
But we didn't buy them

Remember the rocks magma made
Beaten by acid wind
Shaped like hearts
Like ours, cracked in half
Some we held in our hands
Then returned to the earth

Some we could only stare at
In awe
And hold in our hearts

When You Open Your Hand

Is freedom the same as love?
Please say it is
I thought truth was freedom
But it isn't
Truth is pain, an earthly cage
And what are lies?
They feel good
But not in a good way

Like candy or cocaine or a strawberry that tasted
fine when you bit into one side but then you
turned it over and found it fuzzy and white

Lies are love's red herrings
disguised as butterflies
I'm amazed when I see them
I feed them sugar
Keep them captive in my mind
Say, I won't let you go till I die

But if we held anything in our hands
For as long as we did in our minds
That would be insane
We'd put it down and step away

If love is freedom
Then why are there so many damn butterflies
Why do they all look different
But end up the same
How can I be allergic to pollen and stupid
But not to clever or Cupid
Until I've caught them
In a homemade pain-cage
Wings fluttering in my palms
Feels good
And not...
Maybe the question I'm asking is wrong
Maybe instead of 'what' is freedom
I should be asking
When

Do You Speak Any Other Languages?

Speaking languages means less to me than being
fluent in poetry
You feel it instead
Like warm light with a lot of breath
Like walking under trees wondering, is that
rain?
Like infatuation at midnight that burns and fades
A dream you want to stay in
But it's just a dream babe
Still — Feels good anyway
You don't always have to know or explain
You can put pencil to paper and smile
And wait
Pirouette in place and hope the next drop hits
you're tongue
Wouldn't that be something?
That's how poetry feels
Dancing under trees
Waiting for the rain

You Have Beautiful Eyes

I haven't felt the fear of being a woman in
awhile
But today I turned a corner in broad daylight
Met a silver smile in a tatted face
Twice my size
"You have beautiful eyes" he said
Three or four of his strides
Ten or more of mine away
I don't want to die
Or worse
Avert your beautiful eyes
Lock the car and check the mirror twice
Then drive back to
"why can't he love me right?"
Is it because he's never had to ask
"Will you walk me home?"
Or "Will you watch my drink?
Or is it that my eyes are just too beautiful
To see through lies

It Feels Like the End

To see you
Suddenly tiny
And in an instant
All you were missing
Was breath

I can't wait until
Gentle arms lower me
And a fistful of dirt
Into the beginning
When we meet again

I Fell Farthest

I liked knowing
The name of your heart
A word easy to memorize

Don't leave--
Running back to your lips I come
Life without them was my funeral

My worst compulsion was your body in full
bloom
I fell to touch that what if of love
But not you

Alchemy

She ripped my necklace off getting in the car
later that day
In four-year-old fury and rage
In the bubbling up of everything she can't say
Disappointment on my face spun her out again
And with my bones bleeding strength, heartbeat
at half speed
All I could do was toss the beads I caught like
confetti
To paint the floor when I drove away
Like marbles in a tray
A visual soliloquy
That's the kind of art I make these days

It's Grief

The opposite of courage isn't fear
Courage means you're afraid
But you're pushing fear aside to fly
Grief means you've given fear the reigns
And consent to drive
Right into the closest lake
Trick you into feeling safe
So as the water trickles in
You sit and wait to suffocate

Real As The Moon

I've been so many faces I can't recall them all
One would make you scurry
One would make you howl
Each subtle turn changing my entire landscape
But it's not so easy to keep turning and changing
I've changed so much they'd yell "witch" if they
knew
They already say the moon isn't real and the
earth is flat
But if that's true, what exactly IS real to you?
The touch of someone's skin?
The heat
The sweat
The grip
It's not, you know
It's electrostatic repulsion

Feeling is as real as
The beginning and end of a rainbow
Seen from the ground
You think plants aren't making sound
But you don't have the capacity to understand
You think trees don't have mothers
And their greatest isn't yours too?
That mycelium doesn't dance

Or fall in love with you?

Were you aware that flowers find you beautiful
Plant themselves on purpose
Draw your likeness with their roots
Tell the whole underworld about your pursuits
What makes you flourish
What kills you
They call you their favorite
Then send the sound of your laugh
Through a network to a ste
On the other side of the earth
A subtle gift, translation:
"I like you"

I've had so many faces
Which one is real?
The one that brought out your shadows
Or the one that showed her depths to you
Of all the faces I've been I do have a favorite
And it's always the same
The one I am right now
She's as real as they get babe

Last Light

Every full moon
I miss you less
See more of myself
Instead of what if's
I've stopped bartering with the sky
to bring you back
I'm getting used to the black ceiling
Shining bright on my own
Almost forgotten the feeling
Of first light on the horizon
Celestial and slow
But I remember the loss
When time stopped
My breath caught
In the back of my throat
And you — gone
Under a full moon
With no stars left to wish on

Sunny Spots

The sun passes through my house at dusk
Like a lover I once knew
Moving swiftly room to room
Gingerly touching edges of furniture
Glinting off doorknobs
Illuminating dust
And darkness I'd forgotten all about
Painting my walls with shadows
Briefly, makes everything look anew
Then leaves —
And in the morning
Peeks between the blinds
Begs to come inside
The moment I oblige is made of magic
I lose all my senses
I am no longer human
I am blind, I am wild
Climbing out of woe again
Warmth runs over everything
Like sugar in my veins
Like fingers through my hair
Tickling the tip of my nose
Sweetly tracing my earlobes

I can tell you all the best spots in my house

If you're looking for a sun-kissed tryst
Maybe love is just
Photosynthesis

What I mean when I say: I want to live exquisitely

Some days still defeat me
Break me
Bruise me
I'm running nowhere
Chasing a time-storm moving with no mercy
Wanting everything
But watching possibilities pruning
One by one
Like petals I plucked
And tucked in my pockets
To keep a memory
Eventually
They disappear too

Some days still complete me
I find a piece of my puzzle-self
I didn't know was missing
The stars arrange and suddenly
I am not afraid of anything
Magic eyes reveal patterns
I am the earth
Spinning in cosmic poetry
Milky in the way
She sweeps the corridor of space

Exactly where and when I need to be
Finally
Aligned with sun and moon

And if I'm lucky
Some days still ignite me
They're few and far between
But they surprise me
Like a laugh escaping timid lips
Excite me like the kiss
I've been dreaming of
Light me up
Like bioluminescency in darkness
A fiery spark with a long fuse
And a big bang
That's over
All too soon

God is a Woman

What did father-figures teach you?
Here's what I learned:
Silence is safest
Rage is dangerous and unattractive
From a woman it deserves abandonment
And impunity if from a man
Thought I'd stopped self-harming
But self-restraint cuts you up just as bad
So I will sing, I will dance
What did mother-figures teach you?
Here's what I learned:
How to smuggle anger in my bones
Let it secretly implode
Solidify in veins like obsidian
Make beautiful stakes to hang
By my own two hands
But being a martyr doesn't matter
If I'm sacrificing me for me
So I will weep, I will rage

I've been walking on glass lately
Instead of eggshells, petals, or dirt
I'd prefer a bed of nails - you don't know about
glass until it hurts
I've been sleeping in the shards

They bleed into my dreams
Soon they'll all be stuck in me
Like jewelry
I'll glisten
They'll say: How daring! How pretty!
And no one will know the pain I'm in except me
Why is it always "Girl Shedding Glass Pieces"?
Or "Girl Sheds Tears of Glass"?
Don't Google that
Unless you want to see what it's like to swallow
lies
I'll save you time: they pour out your eyes and
into your hand
Don't tell me my dermatitis is artifacta
When clearly it was a man

I remember the first time I had good sex
Because it was more than that - it was good love
The world came alive (pun intended)
Everything felt fresh to my senses, no
occurrence was an annoyance
Nothing could irritate me or piss me off
I had been filled with whole trusting pleasure
Safety without bounds
Synaptic gaps blasted by oxytocin, drowned in
dopamine
Hot blood cycled through me so well all the
emotional gunk and stagnation had been flushed
from my system

Airways open and warm, lymph flowing, fascia
free from tension
I was gliding through life
No, I was life - the creator fully realized
God is a woman after great sex
You can't convince me otherwise

I was Goddess
Sparking, crackling with energy
Ready to pour the love I'd just been filled with --
The slow tender way it started, the heaving
chaotic blaze it became
The blissful waves ending in explosive
crescendo followed by euphoric rest
"The little death" as they say --
I was ready to pour that love back into every
single person I'd ever met
I was Goddess
But she comes with more than just pleasure (pun
intended)
She comes with the weight of the world
It was dripping on me, heavy and warm like oil
pouring and I tried to hold it in my hands but I
couldn't contain it
It slipped through my fingers, I could only
witness it pass
Then I began to paint with it, my body, my walls
I could slide in it and dance
I could use the medium to travel back to bliss

Oh, the fleet of Goddess
Of the moments, the movement of everything
It's all just breath bated
In -- pause
Out -- pause
Do it again, and again, and again, don't stop
I bet genocide wouldn't exist if everyone was
having good sex

So it's the morning after making great love
Body buzzing, you've got all the energy to craft
a fruit plate and heart-shaped pancakes - okay,
one that looks like Mickey Mouse, but that's on
purpose I promise
You want the music loud because you can't hear
the sound over all the feelings
And you have a compulsion to sing at the top of
your lungs, neighbors be damned
Your hips are moving to the beat in your
grandmother's apron you've never worn before
now
Your hands fly like fairies chopping juicy pieces
of melon
You're sucking the pink drops from your
fingertips and shamelessly sharing a bit with
your lover
Then back to chopping and and dancing (((DAT
DAT DAT)))
Like a madwoman (((DAT DAT DAT)))

Then (((WHACK)))

That wasn't the flesh of fruit
And at first you can't breathe, can't see
Did you lose a finger
Or your feelings
It's the same sensation if you ask me
Did you slam the door
Or did he
Was it his fist through the plaster or your chest
It's like you're watching your mother get thrown
against the wall and wrestled to the floor all over
again except
Instead of standing on the sidelines you're up
close behind sad eyes
No one tells you violence is genetic
They just ask:
Did you throw the phone at the wall or at him
because of what he said
Did you smash the potted plants to make a mess
or a point without sense
Did he chuck the bike across the room because
you forgot to load the dryer or because his dad
shot himself in the head
Does he demand sex every day because he's a
fiend
Or because he's afraid of the empty womb you
now carry after they murdered your baby at

20-weeks-old still while it was still inside your
belly
Hard to say

Pain is complicated
You can't numb it with meds and expect it not to
be there the next day
By the way pain and grief are not the same
Grief you can collect and hang proudly to
decorate your soul
Pain is that glint of light on those colorful glass
baubles of grief
Twinkling in the night when it's dark and quiet
And altogether it's sort of beautiful

I think the measure of wisdom is not how much
you've lived
But how often you die
Yes, an empty synapse hurts every time, but it
means you're alive

One last story:
I met a man sometime later in life and when I
told him I used to work for hospice he asked
"How?"
They all do
I said, "It's not so bad always thinking about
death. People dying are very light. They want to

hear jokes, sing songs, listen and talk without
being fake. It's nice."
He said, "I don't believe there's anything after
life."
"That would make death difficult," I replied
"What do you think?" he asked
"Well, I don't know if you've ever seen a birth,
but it's quite..." I paused here, looking for the
word
Until he found it for me: "Magical" he said
"Yes," I agreed
He nodded and smiled and said "I know, I've
been just outside the room."
I continued, "The more magical births you see,
the more you're convinced there is SOME thing
before life. It's the same with death."
Then our conversation turned to the remarkable
animal births he'd seen on TV
And because he'd only been so far, that's where I
had to leave him
Just outside the room

Sisters, you'll have to excuse him
He's never known bloodshed like you
He's never looked at his own hands in a bath of
red
Or felt fear slowly creeping down his leg

He's never worried about how quickly the shame
stains and he doesn't know that hot water sets
the proteins
He can't remember inside the womb and he's
only ever been just outside the room
So he'll never know true darkness, unless you
show him babe
Show him - sing, dance, weep, rage
Don't let him get away thinking he's got it made
Thinking he understands life
Because God is a white man waiting in a
heavenly room just outside

No, God is a woman after great sex covered in
oil and regret
And all the rest of the universe is what comes
next (pun intended)
You can't convince me otherwise

www.ingramcontent.com/pod-product-compliance
Lightning Source LLC
LaVergne TN
LVHW010914200726
843509LV00013B/1940